Tellwell Talent
www.tellwell.ca

ISBN
978-1-77941-029-0 (Hardcover)
978-1-77941-028-3 (Paperback)
978-1-77941-031-3 (eBook)

TORTOISE GOES TO THE VET

RADHA – INDIAN STAR TORTOISE

WRITTEN & ILLUSTRATED
BY
PARIMALASRI DOCKTOR

My dad and mom think that I am the most beautiful girl.
Dad calls me "Rod," short for Radha. I am almost five years old.

Mom and Dad hand-feed me every day since I cannot grab food well with my crooked beak.

When I try, I drop most of my food on the ground and cannot pick it up.

Ever since I was a baby, my beak has been overgrown on one side, making my mouth crooked.

My friend Krishna eats on his own most of the time.

Mom tried trimming my beak, but Dad was afraid that this might hurt me.

Mom said to Dad, "Radha needs to see a vet to get her beak trimmed."

Dad was still afraid, but I think Mom was trying to help me.

We took a bus ride to My City Vet.

The nurse took my
weight, and the doctor
came to examine me.

They thought I was
cool since I can
skateboard.

The doctor said to Mom and Dad,
"On the day of the procedure,
I will give her some medicine to make her go to sleep.
Then it will be easy for me to trim and file her beak."

We went home. I told Krishna that I was scared.

The big day came.

Mom and Dad left me with the nurse and went home, since they were not supposed to stay with me in the hospital.

I didn't want to be alone with the strangers.

The doctor gave me some medicine and I didn't like it.

I didn't want my beak trimmed or filed!

I wanted to go home. I wanted my dad.

I would not come out of my shell until my mom and dad came!

Then, I heard my doctor say on the telephone, "Radha will not come out of her shell, and I have tried everything I could."

Quickly, Mom and Dad came. I heard my dad and mom calling me, but I would not come out. Not here, anyway.

We went home.

Dad was very worried that something bad had happened to me. He said, "Rod, come out and look at me. We love you the way you are."

Then Mom said, "Your friend Krishna is here."

Now, I had to come out of my shell to tell Krishna about my adventures at the vet's office.

He thought I was exaggerating

and laughed.

Since my trip to the vet, I let my mom trim my beak.

Dad is not afraid anymore.

I can grab some food, like cucumber and squash by myself, but I still like my mom or dad to feed me dinner every day.

Guess what?

I was Pet of the Month at My City Vet.

I am just the way my family likes me: beautiful.

Let us play a couple of games:

1. How many pictures of me, do you see in the puzzle?

2. Help me find my way to the Vet's office, please

 → →

About Indian Star Tortoises

Lifespan: 30 - 80 years

Adult Size: 7 - 12 inches

Habitat: Parts of India, Sri Lanka & Pakistan

Diet : Plant based

Answer to Puzzle 1 : 34

Thank you for being a part of my life
love Radha

Printed in the USA
CPSIA information can be obtained
at www.ICGtesting.com
LVHW070705161023
761142LV00063B/50